DATE DUE		

SCIENCE STARTERS

Magnets and Sparks

Wendy Madgwick

RSVP

**RAINTREE
STECK-VAUGHN**
PUBLISHERS
A Steck-Vaughn Company

Austin, Texas

Titles in this series:
Up in the Air • Water Play • Magnets and Sparks
Super Sound • Super Materials • Light and Dark
Living Things • On the Move

Published by Raintree Steck-Vaughn Publishers, an imprint of Steck-Vaughn Company

Library of Congress Cataloging-in-Publication Data
Madgwick, Wendy.
Magnets and sparks / Wendy Madgwick.
    p.   cm.—(Science Starters)
    Includes bibliographical references and index.
    Summary: Provides instruction for a variety of projects demonstrating the properties and uses of magnets and electricity.
    ISBN 0-8172-5328-9
    1. Magnets—Experiments—Juvenile literature.
    2. Electricity—Experiments—Juvenile literature.
    3. Electric spark—Experiments—Juvenile literature.
    [1. Magnets—Experiments. 2. Electricity—Experiments.
    3. Experiments]
    I. Title. II. Series: Madgwick, Wendy, Science starters.
    QC757.5.M33 1999
    538'.078—dc21   98-14618

Printed in Italy. Bound in the United States.
1 2 3 4 5 6 7 8 9 0 03 02 01 00 99

Words that appear in **bold** in the text are explained in the glossary on page 30.

Illustrations: Catherine Ward/Simon Girling Associates
Photographer: Andrew Sydenham
Picture Acknowledgements: pages 5 and 19 Zefa; page 13 RGS; page 20 TRIP/G. Grieves

Contents

Looking at Magnets and Electricity

This book has lots of fun activities to help you find out about magnets and electricity. Here are some simple rules you should follow before doing an activity.

- Always tell an adult what you are doing and ask if you can do the activity.
- Always read through the activity before you start. Collect the materials you will need. They are listed on page 28.
- Make sure you have enough space to set up your activity.
- Follow the steps carefully and do exactly what you are told.
- Ask an adult to strip the plastic off electrical wires and to help you cut things.
- Watch what happens carefully.
- Take care of your magnets. Try not to drop them. When you are not using them, put a piece of steel across the ends. Or stick your magnets together in pairs.
- Use a 4.5-volt battery with clear terminals for these experiments. **NEVER** use larger batteries or car batteries because these can be dangerous.
- **NEVER TOUCH ELECTRICITY SOCKETS OR PLUGS.**
- Never put a magnet very near a watch, clock, computer or television screen.
- Keep a notebook. Draw pictures or write down what you did and what happened.
- Always clear up when you have finished. Wash your hands.

▶ When **static electricity** passes from one thundercloud to another or to the ground, we see a flash of **lightning**.

Magic Magnets

A magnet is a piece of iron or steel that draws things toward it. We say it **attracts** an object. Let's find out what things a magnet attracts.

Stick or stay?
Collect small things made from different materials as in the picture.

Put the end of the magnet near each object. Which ones stick to the magnet? A magnet attracts things made from steel and iron. It will not attract things made from other materials. It does not attract all metals.

Flying butterfly

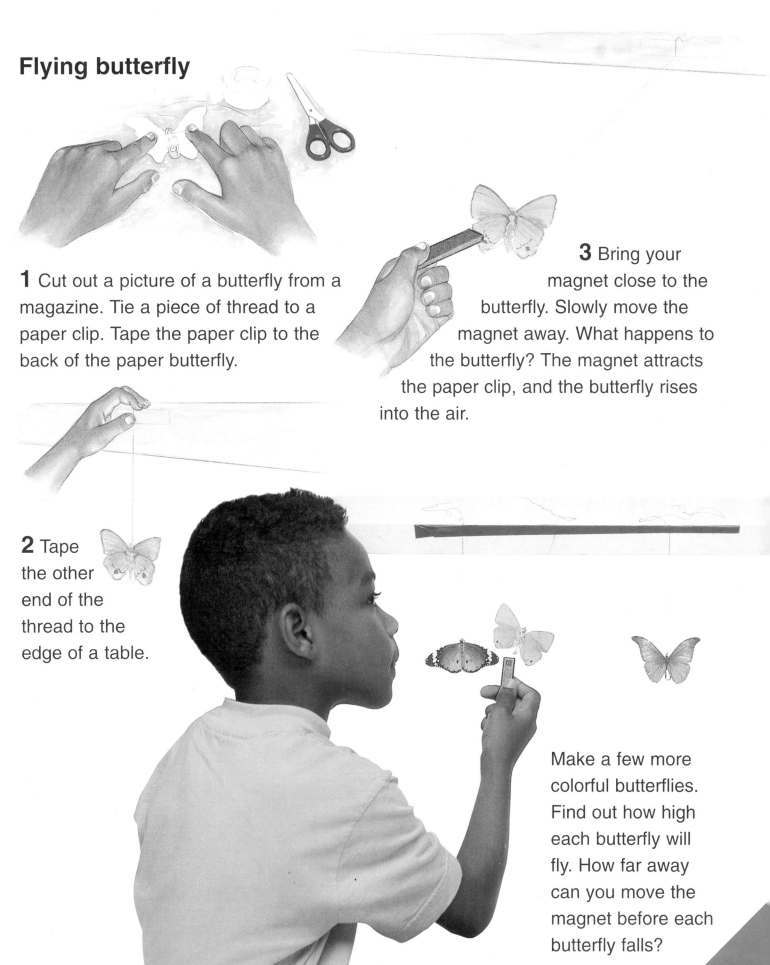

1 Cut out a picture of a butterfly from a magazine. Tie a piece of thread to a paper clip. Tape the paper clip to the back of the paper butterfly.

3 Bring your magnet close to the butterfly. Slowly move the magnet away. What happens to the butterfly? The magnet attracts the paper clip, and the butterfly rises into the air.

2 Tape the other end of the thread to the edge of a table.

Make a few more colorful butterflies. Find out how high each butterfly will fly. How far away can you move the magnet before each butterfly falls?

7

Lift Up!

Some magnets are stronger than others. Strong magnets have more pulling power than weak magnets. How strong are your magnets? Let's find out.

Pulling power

Put some paper clips on a flat surface. Pick up a paper clip with a magnet. How many paper clips can you pick up at one time? Now repeat with a different magnet.

The strongest magnet will pick up the most paper clips.

Let's fish

You can use magnets and paper clips to make a fishing game.

1 Cut out some fish shapes from kitchen foil. Push a paper clip onto each fish.

3 Put the foil fish in a bowl of water. Try to catch the fish with your magnet fishing rod. The player who picks up the most fish is the winner.

2 Tie a piece of thread about 12 in. (30 cm) long to a small magnet. Tie the other end of the thread to a thin stick. Tape it in place.

Move It!

Magnets can attract things through water and through some solid objects.

Sail away

1 Cut a small cork in half lengthwise to make two boats. Draw two sail shapes on cardboard. Cut them out.

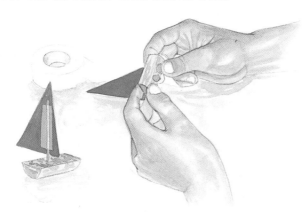

2 Tape a wooden cocktail stick to each sail. Push the pointed end of each stick into the cork halves. Push two drawing pins into the bottom of each cork boat.

3 Tape a magnet to a small ruler or stick.

4 Put a shallow plastic tray on two piles of magazines of the same height. Pour in some water and float your boats.

5 Push the magnet under the tray. Move the magnet around to move your boats.

Diving doll

1 Make a small doll from modeling clay. Press two paper clips into its back, one on top of the other.

2 Put your doll in a jar. Make sure its back is toward the outside of the jar.

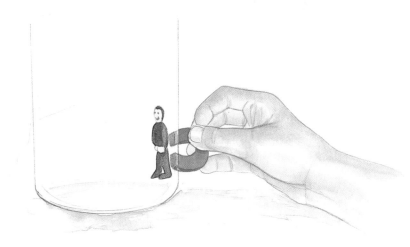

3 Slide a magnet up the side of the jar by the doll. The magnet attracts the paper clips. As you move the magnet it pulls up the doll.

Push or Pull?

Magnets have two ends, or poles.
One end is called the north pole.
The other is called the south pole.

North or south?

You can use a **compass** to find the north pole of a magnet.

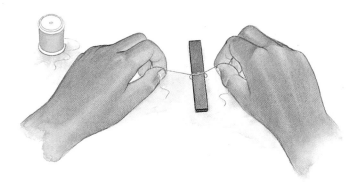

1 Tie a thread around the middle of a magnet.

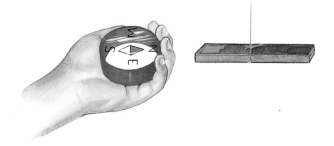

2 Hang the magnet from a table. When the magnet stops moving, use a compass to find which end is pointing north. Paint the north pole red and the south pole green.

3 Bring the north pole of one magnet near the south pole of another magnet.

4 Bring two magnets' north poles near each other. What happens to the magnets?

North and south poles attract each other. The two magnets come together. Like poles **repel** each other. This means that two north poles or two south poles push each other away.

Flying planes

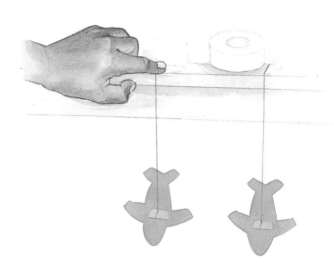

1 Draw two airplane shapes on thick cardboard. Cut them out. Tape a small magnet underneath each plane. The north poles must point to the nose of each plane.

2 Tape a thread 12 inches (30 cm) long to the center of each plane. Hang the planes about 8 inches (20 cm) apart from the side of a table. Make sure they are pointing toward you.

3 Gently tap the nose of one plane toward the nose of the other plane. What happens?
The planes will keep swinging back and forth.

▲ A compass needle always points north. It can help you find your way.

Fancy Fields

A magnet has a special area around it called a **magnetic field**. Inside this field a magnet has pulling power. This field is invisible but we can see it in other ways.

Pretty patterns

2 Tap the paper gently. What happens to the iron filings? The iron filings are attracted to the magnet and form a pattern. This pattern shows what the magnetic field looks like.

1 Put a magnet on a table. Place a sheet of paper over it. Sprinkle some iron filings over the paper.

End to end

What happens to the magnetic field when you bring two magnets together?

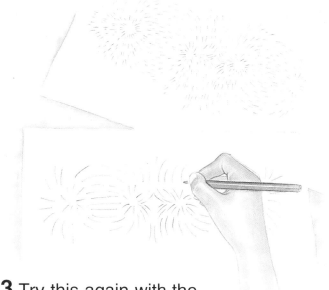

1 Put two magnets on a table. Put one magnet's north pole about 2 in. (5 cm) away from the other's south pole.

2 Put a sheet of paper on top of the magnets. Slowly sprinkle on some iron filings. Tap the paper gently. What pattern do the iron filings make? Draw a picture of the pattern.

3 Try this again with the south poles of the two magnets facing each other. Is the pattern different?

When a north pole faces a south pole, the iron filings form lines between them.

When two south poles face each other, the iron filings bend away from the poles.

On End

When some objects are rubbed together, they build up static electricity. These objects are said to have an **electric charge**.

Hair raising

Make sure your hair is clean and dry. Rub your hair several times with a balloon. Now bring the balloon near your hair. What happens? Your hair should stand on end!

The hair and the balloon become charged with static electricity. Your hair has an opposite charge to the balloon. The charge on your hair is attracted to the charge on the balloon.

Balloon power

Can you make a balloon stick to a wall on its own?

1 Blow up a balloon with a pump. Knot the end. Put the balloon against the wall. Let it go. What happens?

2 Now rub the balloon 20 times with a piece of nylon. Hold the part of the balloon you rubbed against the wall. What happens now?

3 Wet the balloon and rub it with the nylon. Put the balloon against the wall. What happens?

4 Dry the balloon. Rub the balloon 20 times with other dry, clean materials. Try wool, cotton, wood, and kitchen foil. Which materials make the balloon stick to the wall?

Charges and Sparks

Static electricity can build up in an object. It can pass from one object to another as a spark of electricity. It can also leak away.

Move over!

1 Blow up two balloons. Tie a piece of thread to each balloon. Hold up the balloons about 8 in. (20 cm) apart. Do the balloons move?

2 Rub each balloon 20 times with nylon material.

3 Hold up the balloons with the rubbed sides next to each other. What happens?

4 Hold the balloons still for a few seconds. Watch what happens.

The rubbed balloons will move apart. When you leave the balloons the charge leaks away. The balloons fall back down.

Lift off

Can you pick up paper with a pen?

1 Cut some tissue paper into $^1/_2$ in. (1 cm) squares. Put a clean plastic pen near the paper. What happens to the paper?

2 Rub the pen hard five times with nylon material. Put it near the paper. What happens now?

3 Rub the pen 20 times. Does it pick up more paper?

4 Leave the pen for two minutes. Can you pick up as much paper as before?

The more you rub the pen, the more paper it will pick up. After two minutes, you will not be able to pick up as much paper.

◀ Lightning is a flash of static electricity that passes from a thundercloud to another cloud or to the ground.

Power Light

When electricity flows along a wire we call it an **electric current**. Electricity is used to run machines. It can be stored in a **battery**. Batteries are used to make things work.

▲ The electricity in your home flows from a **power plant** along big wires. Do you know which machines in this picture use electricity?

Battery power

These things use batteries to make them work. Can you think of other things that use batteries?

Light up

Let's see how a flashlight works.

1 Look at a flashlight. Make sure the switch is off. Is the bulb lit?
Ask an adult to help you take the flashlight apart. Look at all the parts.

2 Ask an adult to put the flashlight back together. Switch it on. What happens?

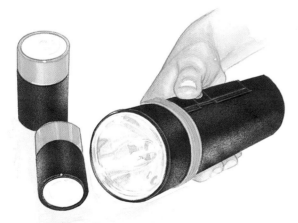

3 Open the end of the flashlight. Take out the batteries. Put the end back on and switch the flashlight on. What happens?

4 Put the batteries back in. Take out the bulb. Put the end back on. Switch on the flashlight. What happens?

Your flashlight will only light up when the battery and bulb are there and the switch is on.

21

Wired Up!

The battery, switch, and bulb in a flashlight are connected by wires to make a **circuit**. Electricity flows from the battery along wires and lights the bulb.

Light circuits

Make a circuit to light a bulb.

1 Take two pieces of electric wire 8 in. (20 cm) long with bare ends. Wind each end around a paper clip.

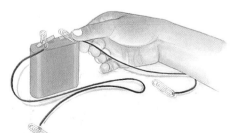

2 Clip a piece of wire to each battery terminal.

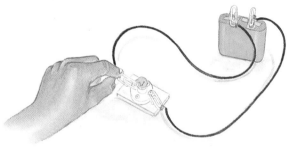

3 Put the bulb in the bulb holder. Attach pieces of wire to the bulb holder as shown. Does the bulb light up?

4 Take the wire off one battery terminal. Is the bulb still lit?

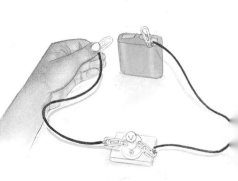

The bulb lights when the circuit is complete.

Keep it steady

1 Remove one wire from your circuit. Attach a paper clip to one end of a piece of wire 10 in. (25 cm) long with bare ends. Clip the wire to the free battery terminal. Wind the other end around a metal hanger.

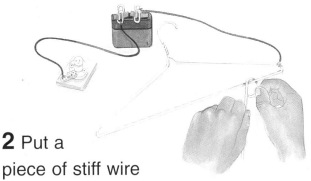

2 Put a piece of stiff wire 10 in. (25 cm) long through the middle of the hanger. Bend one end of the wire into a loop around the hanger.

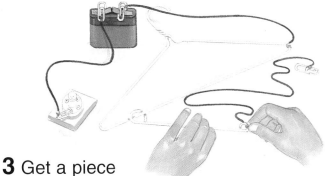

3 Get a piece of wire 16 in. (40 cm) long with bare ends. Twist one end of the wire around the free end of the stiff wire.

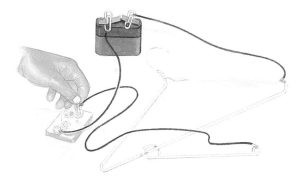

4 Attach the other end of this wire to the bulb holder. Hang up the hanger.

Try to pass the loop along the hanger so they don't touch. If the loop touches the hanger you will complete the circuit and the bulb will light.

Stop or Flow?

Electricity can only flow through certain materials. These are called **conductors**. Materials that do not let electricity flow through them are called **insulators**.

Light the bulb

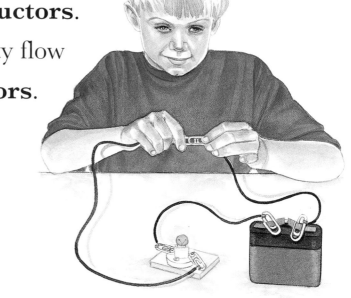

1 Set up a simple circuit as on page 22. Remove one wire from the bulb holder.

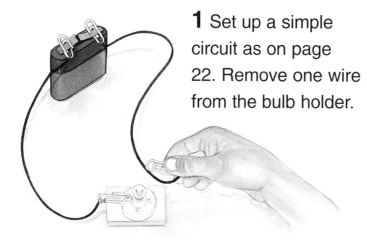

3 Touch the two paper clips together. The bulb should light. If it doesn't, make sure all the connections are tight.

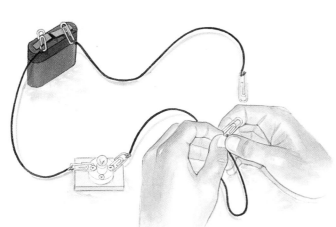

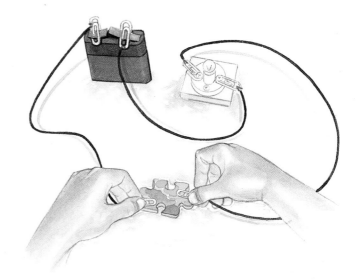

2 Get a piece of wire 6 in. (15 cm) long with bare ends. Put a paper clip on each end. Clip one end to the bulb holder. You should have two free ends of wire.

4 Put the two paper clips on either side of a piece of wood. Touch the wood. Does the bulb light?

5 Collect a cork, a plastic brick, some kitchen foil, a coin, wood, nails, screws, drawing pins, and paper clips. Test each material in turn. Which materials let the bulb light? Which do not?

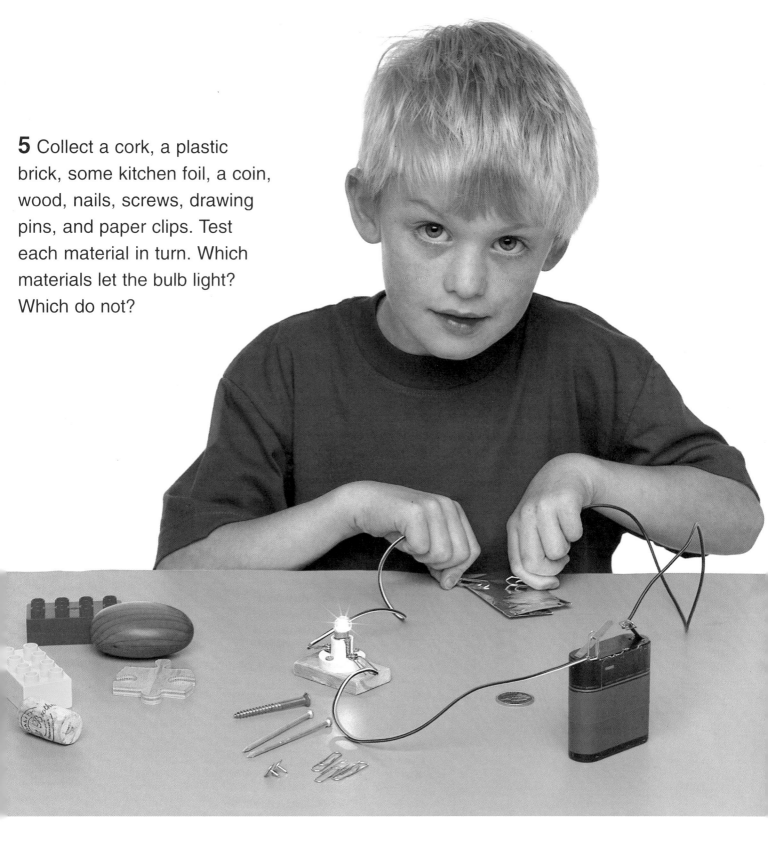

Metals are conductors. They let the electric current through. The bulb lights. Kitchen foil, paper clips, nails, screws, and drawing pins are made of metal.

Wood, plastic, and cork are insulators. They do not let electricity through, so the bulb does not light.

On/Off

When you switch off a flashlight, the circuit is no longer complete. This means the bulb will not light. You can use a switch to turn any electrical circuit on and off.

When you turn an electrical circuit on and off, you can make a light flash. A lighthouse does just that.

Flashing lighthouse

1 Attach two pieces of wire 16 in. (40 cm) long to a bulb holder. Put paper clips on the ends.

2 Roll some thick cardboard into a tube and tape it together. The bulb holder should just fit into the top of the tube. Tape it in place. The wire must be on the outside of the tube.

3 Tape the wire to the outside of the tube. Attach one wire to a terminal.

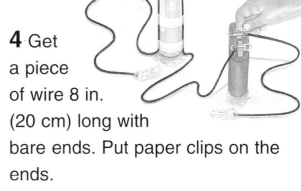

4 Get a piece of wire 8 in. (20 cm) long with bare ends. Put paper clips on the ends.
Attach one end of the wire to the free battery terminal. The two wires with paper clips on the ends make a switch.

5 Cover the tube with some bright paper. Tape it in place. Stand the tube in a box. Put modeling clay around the bottom to make a base.

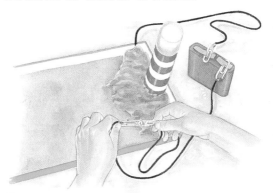

6 Put a small jar over the bulb. Touch the two free paper clips. The bulb should light. Can you make the bulb flash on and off?

Materials you will need

p. 6 Magic Magnets—magnet, plastic brick, kitchen foil, thread reel, iron nail, coin, thread, tape, paper clips, round-ended scissors. Look for pictures of butterflies in a magazine.

p. 8 Lift Up!—paper clips, two magnets, kitchen foil, round-ended scissors, bowl of water, two small magnets, thread, two thin sticks. Ask a friend to join in.

p. 10 Move It!—cork (ask an adult to cut the cork in half), round-ended scissors, cardboard, pencil, two wooden cocktail sticks, four drawing pins, magnet, stick, shallow plastic tray, thick magazines, water, modeling clay, two paper clips, jar, strong magnet.

p. 12 Push or Pull?—thread, two bar magnets, poster paints, compass, thick cardboard, round-ended scissors, two small magnets, tape.

p. 14 Fancy Fields—two bar magnets, paper, iron filings, pencil.

p. 16 On End—balloon, balloon pump, nylon material, water, towel, wool, cotton material, piece of wood, kitchen foil.

p. 18 Charges and Sparks—two balloons, balloon pump, thread, nylon material, tissue paper, round-ended scissors, clean plastic pen.

p. 20 Power Light—flashlight.

p. 22 Wired Up!—35 in. (90 cm) electrical wire, six paper clips, round-ended scissors, battery, bulb, bulb holder, metal coat hanger, 10 in. (25 cm) stiff wire.

p. 24 Stop or Flow?—28 in. (55 cm) electrical wire, six paper clips, round-ended scissors, bulb, bulb holder, battery, objects made from plastic, cotton, wood, metal, cork, and paper.

p. 26 On/Off—3 ft. (1 m) electrical wire, four paper clips, round-ended scissors, battery, bulb, bulb holder, thick cardboard, tape, bright paper, modeling clay, small jar, shallow cardboard box.

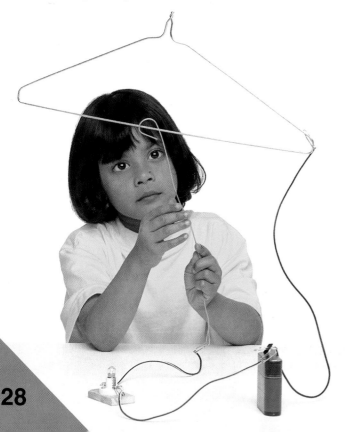

Hints to helpers

Pages 6 and 7

Only certain materials are magnetic. These include some metals, such as iron, nickel, and cobalt and alloys, such as steel. Talk about the uses of magnets, e.g., magnetic catches to keep things closed, compasses, machines for picking up metal.

The magnet will only attract the butterfly as long as it is within its magnetic field. When you move the magnet too far away from the butterfly, it will fall back.

Pages 8 and 9

You can make your own magnets by stroking a magnet along a steel nail from the top to the tip. You should always stroke the nail in the same direction. Normally, the tiny particles that make up the iron nail are pointing in different directions. As you stroke the nail with the magnet, the particles form into lines pointing in the same direction. The nail acts as a magnet as long as the particles stay in line.

The magnets on the end of the stick attract the paper clips so that the fish are picked up. The magnetic force is not blocked by the water, so a magnet can attract the paper clips even through water.

Pages 10 and 11

The magnetic force is not blocked by water, plastic, or glass. The magnet can still attract the metal drawing pins and paper clips.

Pages 12 and 13

Discuss how the earth acts as if there is an enormous bar magnet along its center. A compass needle is a small magnet that lines up with the earth's magnetic field, so it always points north and south. Point out that the earth's magnetic north and south poles are not the same as the geographic north and south poles.

The planes keep on swinging because the north poles repel each other, so the noses swing away from each other. This brings the tails together. The south poles also repel each other, so the tails swing apart. The heads then swing together, so the planes keep swinging. You can use the magnet with its poles marked red and green to find the north poles of your magnets for this experiment.

Pages 14 and 15

No one completely understands the invisible force that surrounds a magnet. The iron filings gather together in regions where the magnetic force is stronger. A lot of filings cluster at the ends of the magnet, where the magnetic force is strongest.

The iron filings form lines between the north and south poles of two magnets because the magnetic fields between the poles join up. Opposite poles attract each other. The iron filings between two south poles bend away from the poles because the magnetic fields push away, or repel, each other.

Pages 16 and 17

Experiments with static electricity are most successful on dry, cold days. When the balloon is rubbed on the child's hair, it gains tiny particles called electrons and develops a negative charge. The hair loses electrons and develops a positive charge. Just as the north and south poles of magnets attract each other, so a negative and a positive charge attract one another. The hair stands on end as it is attracted to the balloon.

When you rub the balloon with the nylon, it becomes charged with static electricity. The charge on the balloon makes it stick to the wall. When the balloon is wet, the static electricity cannot build up, so the balloon does not stick to the wall. Some materials, such as nylon and wool, build up a static charge very well. Others, like cotton and wood, do not.

A good way for a child to see and hear static electricity is by wearing a nylon shirt under a woolen sweater. A static charge will build up between the sweater and the shirt. If you undress in a dark room and watch carefully in a mirror, as you pull off the sweater, you should hear a crackle and see some tiny sparks fly.

Pages 18 and 19

When the balloons are rubbed with the nylon, they both develop a negative charge. Like charges repel each other, so the two balloons push apart.

When you rub the pen with nylon, the pen becomes charged and attracts the tissue paper. The more you rub the pen, the greater the charge on it will be. If you wait, the charge on the pen will lessen and it will not attract the tissue paper so strongly.

Lightning is produced when static electricity builds up in a thundercloud. The top of the cloud becomes positively charged while the bottom of the cloud carries a negative charge. The negative charges are strongly attracted to the ground. They leap from cloud to cloud or to the ground as flashes of lightning. The heat from the flash makes the air expand suddenly, making a loud thunder clap.

Pages 20 and 21

The picture of a kitchen shows a microwave, oven, stove, and electric kettle. All of these are powered by electricity. There are electric lights in the ceiling as well.

Discuss why all the parts of a flashlight are needed to make a complete circuit.

Pages 22 and 23

Discuss what happens when a circuit is complete. The electricity flows from the batteries through the wires to the bulb. If a wire is not connected, the circuit is not complete, so the electricity cannot flow to the bulb.

Pages 24 and 25

Discuss the use of conductors and insulators of electricity. For example, copper electric wires are good conductors of electricity. The plastic coverings on electrical wires are good insulators.

Discuss the uses of electrical switches in the home. For example, when you turn on a light, the switch closes a gap in the electrical circuit. This allows the current to flow through the bulb and light it. When you turn off the light, the switch opens the gap and breaks the circuit. So the electricity cannot flow, and the bulb does not light.

Pages 26 and 27

The light can be made to flash on and off by touching or separating the paper clips and making or breaking the circuit.

Discuss other uses of flashing lights, such as security alarms, hazard lights, etc.

Glossary

Attracts Draws or pulls toward. A magnet pulls magnetic objects such as iron or steel toward it.

Battery This has special chemicals inside it. They work together to make or store small amounts of electricity. A battery stops working when the chemicals are used up.

Circuit An electrical circuit is a path of wires. An electric current can only flow around the circuit when it is complete.

Compass An instrument with a needle that always points north–south. A compass helps you find your way. The needle is a magnet. Its tip is its north pole, which always points to the north.

Conductors Materials that allow electricity or heat to pass through them.

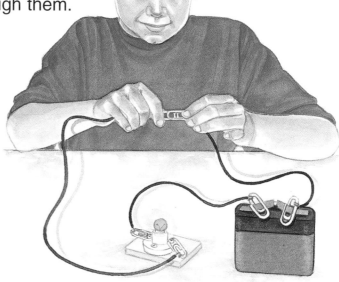

Electric charge An amount of electricity. There are two types of electric charge – a positive charge and a negative charge. Objects with opposite charges attract each other. Objects with the same electric charge repel each other.

Electric current A flow of electric charge through a material. Electricity flows through wires rather like water flows through a pipe.

Insulators Materials that do not allow electricity or heat to pass through them.

Lightning A huge spark of electricity that occurs during a thunderstorm. It is made when a static electric charge builds up in a cloud. The charge passes from cloud to cloud or from a cloud to the ground. We see it as a flash of light.

Magnetic field The space around a magnet in which the magnetic force can be felt.

Power plant A building that makes electricity from other forms of energy such as coal and gas.

Repel To push away from. In magnets, it means the pushing apart of magnets when two like poles are brought near one another. This is called repulsion.

Static electricity A kind of electricity in which the electric charge stays still or is static.

Switch An object that breaks or completes an electric circuit.

Further reading

Gibson, Gary. *Playing with Magnets/With Easy to Make Scientific Projects* (Science for Kids). Brookfield, CT: Copper Beech, 1995.

Glover, David. *Batteries, Bulbs, and Wires: Science Facts and Experiments* (Young Discoverers). New York: Kingfisher Books, 1995.

Rowe, Julian. *Amazing Magnets* (First Science). Danbury, CT: Children's Press, 1997.

Whalley, Margaret. *Experiment with Magnets and Electricity.* Minneapolis, MN: Lerner Group, 1993.

Index

attracts 6–7, 12, 16, 29, 30

batteries 4, 20–21, 22–23, 27, 29, 30
bulb 21, 22–23, 24–25, 26–27, 29

circuit 22–3, 24, 26, 29, 30, 31
compass 12, 13, 29, 30
conductors 24–25

electric charge 16, 18–19, 29, 30, 31
electric current 20, 25, 29, 30
electricity 4, 18, 20, 22, 24, 29, 30, 31

flashlight 21, 26, 29

insulators 24–25, 29, 30
iron 6, 29, 30
iron filings 14–15, 29

lighthouse 26–27
lightning 4, 19, 29, 31

magnetic field 14–15, 29, 31
magnets 4, 6–7, 8–9, 10–11, 12–13, 14–15, 29, 30, 31
metals 6, 25, 29

north pole 12–13, 15, 29, 30

poles 12–13, 15, 29
power plant 20, 31

repels 12, 29, 30, 31
repulsion 31

south pole 12, 15, 29
static electricity 4, 16, 18–19, 29, 31
steel 4, 6, 29, 30
switch 21, 26–27, 29, 31